In *The Gospel Precisely,* attention to the heartbe about Jesus as king, about Jesus fulfilling the story, about Jesus as David's Messiah. It's about Jesus over and over. This book takes the best of Bates's previous work and makes it even more accessible. Bravo!

— **Scot X. McKnight**, author of *The King Jesus Gospel*; Professor of New Testament, Northern Seminary

When people talk about the gospel today, I think of that wise saying from Inigo Montoya, "You keep using that word. I do not think it means what you think it means." The New Testament authors knew about alternative gospels in the Roman world, yet they claimed the word "gospel" for something far better. Christians talk about preaching, presenting, and living the gospel, but we urgently need more precision. Matthew Bates has done the church a service by giving us accessible guidance. Heartily recommended!

— **Jonathan Storment**, author of *How to Start a Riot*; Preaching Minister, Pleasant Valley Church of Christ, Little Rock, AR

The gospel has been more of a lightning rod in American culture than good news. Bates has removed the veneer of cultural Christianity from the gospel so it can be good news to those Jesus came to save. *The Gospel Precisely* delivers biblical depth at a grassroots level with a healthy helping of practical pastoral coaching. Thank you, Matthew Bates

— **Mark E. Moore**, author of *Core 52*; Teaching Pastor, Christ's Church of the Valley, Phoenix, AZ

Dr. Bates has provided a clear and accessible explanation of the glorious and beautiful gospel. By setting the gospel into the biblical context of the kingdom of God, Bates has enabled us to see what it means to find life and salvation through following Christ the king.

— **Jonathan T. Pennington**, author of *Reading the Gospels Wisely*; New Testament Professor, The Southern Baptist Theological Seminary

What could be better than the gospel—presented with clarity, exactness, and passion? Matthew Bates has provided that with *The Gospel Precisely*. You will not merely enjoy this study; you will grow in your ability to love, serve, and declare Christ with confidence and accuracy.

— **Chuck Sackett**, Leadership & Preaching Team, Madison Park Christian Church, Quincy, IL; Professor of Preaching, Lincoln Christian Seminary

There is a desperate need for the church to recenter on the gospel. Matthew Bates has provided Christians with a fantastic tool to learn why Jesus's kingship is the heart of the gospel and how to proclaim it. Are you an everyday gospel-loving Christian? A leader? Teacher? Missionary? Pastor? This book is for you. With its clear writing and helpful review questions, *The Gospel Precisely* is an excellent study for individuals or church small groups. The answers that Matthew Bates provides might surprise you!

— **Haley Goranson Jacob**, author of *Conformed to the Image of His Son*; Assistant Professor of Theology, Whitworth University

MATTHEW W. BATES

THE REAL LIFE THEOLOGY SERIES

THE
GOSPEL
PRECISELY

SURPRISINGLY GOOD NEWS
ABOUT JESUS CHRIST
THE KING

4

R E N Ǝ W.org

*The Gospel Precisely: Surprisingly Good News About Jesus Christ
the King*
Copyright © 2021 by Matthew W. Bates

Requests for information should be sent via e-mail to Renew. Visit
Renew.org for contact information.

ISBN (paperback) 978-1-949921-66-3
ISBN (Mobi) 978-1-949921-67-0
ISBN (ePub) 978-1-949921-68-7

*Cover and interior design by Harrington Interactive Media
(harringtoninteractive.com)*

Printed in the United States of America

For Dr. Roger Mohrlang,
Professor Emeritus of Theology, Whitworth University

In gratitude for your teaching
and embodiment of the gospel.
It changed my life.

CONTENTS

GENERAL EDITORS' NOTE

Jesus' rescuing kingship is the best imaginable news. The Bible teaches us that this gospel, or "good news," is the essential message for our salvation and lives. At Renew.org Network, we believe that "the Jesus you preach, the gospel you uphold, and the faith you coach will determine the disciple you will get."

Matthew W. Bates is the ideal author to teach us about the gospel. He is an award-winning author. His popular books include *Gospel Allegiance* (Brazos, 2019); *Salvation by Allegiance Alone* (Baker Academic, 2017); and *The Birth of the Trinity* (Oxford University Press, 2015). Bates has earned an advanced degree in biblical studies from a leading Protestant seminary (MCS, Regent College) and from a top Catholic university (PhD, University of Notre Dame). He is a Protestant by conviction, but serves as Associate Professor of Theology at a religiously diverse Catholic institution,

Quincy University. He has practical experience teaching, sharing, and seeking to live out the gospel. Bates also co-founded and co-hosts the popular *OnScript* podcast (OnScript.study). He enjoys hiking, baseball, and chasing around his seven children. You can connect with him on Facebook or Twitter (@MatthewWBates), or visit his author page at MatthewWBates.com.

This book expounds on the section from the Renew.org Leaders' Faith Statement called "The Gospel":

> We believe God created all things and made
> human beings in his image, so that we could enjoy
> a relationship with him and each other. But we lost
> our way, through Satan's influence. We are now
> spiritually dead, separated from God. Without
> his help, we gravitate toward sin and self-rule. The
> gospel is God's good news of reconciliation. It was
> promised to Abraham and David and revealed in
> Jesus' life, ministry, teaching, and sacrificial death
> on the cross. The gospel is the saving action of the
> triune God. The Father sent the Son into the world
> to take on human flesh and redeem us. Jesus came
> as the promised Messiah of the Old Testament.
> He ushered in the kingdom of God, died for our
> sins according to Scripture, was buried, and was
> raised on the third day. He defeated sin and death
> and ascended to heaven. He is seated at the right

hand of God as Lord and he is coming back for his disciples. Through the Spirit, we are transformed and sanctified. God will raise everyone for the final judgment. Those who trusted and followed Jesus by faith will not experience punishment for their sins and separation from God in hell. Instead, we will join together with God in the renewal of all things in the consummated kingdom. We will live together in the new heaven and new earth where we will glorify God and enjoy him forever.

*See the full Network Faith Statements at the end of this book.

Support Scriptures: Genesis 1–3; Romans 3:10–12, 7:8–25; Genesis 12:1–3 & Galatians 3:6–9; Isaiah 11:1–4; 2 Samuel 7:1–16; Micah 5:2–4; Daniel 2:44–45; Luke 1:33; John 1:1–3; Matthew 4:17; 1 Corinthians 15:1–8; Acts 1:11; 2:36; 3:19–21; Colossians 3:1; Matthew 25:31–32; Revelation 21:1ff; Romans 3:21–26.

The following tips might help you use this book more effectively (and the other books in the *Real Life Theology* series):

1. *Five questions, answers, and Scriptures.* We framed this book around five key questions with five short answers and five notable Scriptures. This format provides clarity, making it easier to commit crucial information to memory. This format also enables the books in the *Real Life Theology* series to support our catechism. Our catechism is a series of fixed questions and answers for instruction in church or home. In all, the series has fifty-two questions, answers, and key Scriptures. This particular book focuses on the five that are most pertinent to the gospel.

2. *Personal reflection.* At the end of each chapter are six reflection questions. Each chapter is short and intended for everyday people to read and then process. The questions help you to engage the specific teachings and, if you prefer, to journal your practical reflections.

3. *Discussion questions.* The reflection questions double as discussion-group questions. Even if you do not write down the answers, the questions can be used to stimulate group conversation.

4. *Summary videos.* You can find three to seven-minute video teachings that summarize the book, as well as each chapter, at Renew.org. These short videos can function as standalone teachings. But for groups or group leaders using the book, they can also be used to launch discussion of the reading.

May God use this book to fuel faithful and effective disciple making in your life and church.

For King Jesus,
Bobby Harrington and Daniel McCoy
General Editors, *Real Life Theology* series

INTRODUCTION

I don't intend to waste your time. You're busy. But when a message is urgent, we go to great lengths to catch attention—sparkles, flashing lights, loudspeakers, threats, extravagant promises. Then the message is delivered clearly and concisely.

Make no mistake about it. I have the privilege of relaying the most important announcement of all time: God's own good news for the world, the gospel as presented in Scripture. But sorry. I'm fresh out of glitter. You'll need to settle for the unadorned gospel. Since he is the God of the manger and of the cross, we can trust that God is content to reveal himself in non-flashy ways. Got ears? You'll hear.

"No bells and whistles" does not mean no surprises, though. For example, in our modern world of voting, consensus, and representative government, who would dream that *a king* is

WHO WOULD DREAM THAT *A KING* IS GOD'S ULTIMATE GOOD NEWS?

God's ultimate good news? Doesn't kingship inevitably lead to tyranny? And who would dare to imagine that the ideal king would turn out to be a man *crucified* by the government as a traitor? God's ways are shocking.

The surprises don't stop there. The contemporary church's insufficient grasp of the gospel's framework, as the Bible presents it, means that a basic presentation will offer fresh insights for most. Indeed, since I have led pastors and church leaders through numerous Scripture-based studies of the gospel, I can say with confidence: those who think they know the gospel best are frequently the most surprised by its true shape, content, boundaries, and purposes.

Given the gospel confusion prevalent today, how can we make sure our grip on it is firm? There are four ways. First, give pride of place to Scripture's own summaries. Second, discover how the gospel fits into God's wider story and purposes. Third, differentiate between the gospel itself and closely related ideas such as forgiveness, repentance, and faith. Finally, since we learn most fully when we disciple others, be prepared to share the good news. We'll take up these tasks in the chapters that follow.

Precision is needed. Bridges, such as the Tacoma Narrows, have collapsed due to inaccurate engineering calculations. How much more is at stake here? The gospel remains at the heart of the church, beating for the sake of the world. We dare not get it wrong. That means this study, drawing from the Bible, will be exacting. Those eager for more can consult lengthier books that I and others have written on the gospel and salvation (see the final section for recommended reading).

The result? Surprisingly good news worth sharing: *the gospel precisely*.

1

WHAT IS THE GOSPEL?

Answer: Jesus is the saving king. He preexisted with God the Father. In accordance with God's promises, Jesus became human in the line of David, died for our sins, was buried, was resurrected on the third day, was seen, was installed as king at God's right hand, sent the Spirit, and will return to rule.

For what I received I passed on to you as of first importance: that Christ died for our sins according to the Scriptures, that he was buried, that he was raised on the third day according to the Scriptures.
— 1 Corinthians 15:3–4

We need the real gospel. Urgently. There are many false gospels. These are cultural stories about how to achieve full human flourishing. They are not overtly called "gospels," but because they promise to result in a fulfilled life, people adopt them as their version of life's good news. But these false gospels don't deliver. They leave people hurt, broken, and lifeless. They are counterfeits.

Since these false gospels blend pop culture with a spiritual sensibility, you'll hear some of them proclaimed in churches. Hopefully not in yours. They will tell you that God wants you to be rich, healthy, attractive, and in control of your future. They'll proclaim that God desires you to be successful in your career, athletic, and smart. They might promise that you'll find your soulmate, or if not, at least trendy friends.

These pseudo-gospels will nearly always encourage you to undertake a journey of "self-discovery" (that is, selfish discovery) to find out who you truly are: *I've gotta be free to be me*. When someone questions your self-centered journey, you'll be encouraged to jettison your relationship with them by labeling "toxic" anyone who won't unconditionally affirm who you are becoming. Those who disagree with your vision for yourself are canceled.

But there is one thing false gospels will never ask you to do. This is how you can most easily spot the fraud. They will *never* consistently encourage you toward a cross-shaped allegiance to Jesus and his kingdom. The goal will never be the transformation of you (and those around you) into his suffering-for-others-yet-glorified image.

The more precise we are in our grasp of the gospel, the more readily we can avoid false gospels, embrace the true one, and share it effectively. If you want to know *the gospel precisely*, the best way to achieve this is to explore Bible passages that intentionally summarize it.[1]

JESUS IS THE CHRIST

HIDDEN IN PLAIN SIGHT. So obvious that it is usually missed. Scripture most frequently summarizes the gospel simply by identifying *Jesus as the Christ*. For example, "Every day in the temple and from house to house, they did not cease teaching and gospeling, 'The Christ is Jesus'" (Acts 5:42, AT). English doesn't have a verb for "gospel" activity. But in the original Greek of the New Testament, the noun *euangelion* ("gospel," "good news") has a corresponding verb, *euangelizō* ("to gospel"). To make it clear where gospel activity is in view, I've translated it "gospeling." The early church was continually gospeling, "The Christ is Jesus."

Numerous passages summarize the gospel or gospel-activity with the claim that Jesus is the Christ:

- "Now those who were scattered went about *gospeling* the word. Philip went down to the city of Samaria and *proclaimed to them the Christ*" (Acts 8:4–5, AT);
- "Yet Saul . . . baffled the Jews living in Damascus by *proving that Jesus is the Messiah*" (Acts 9:22);
- "Paul . . . reasoned with them from the Scriptures, explaining and proving that it was necessary for *the Christ* to suffer and to rise from the dead, and saying, '*This is the Christ, this Jesus, whom I am proclaiming to you*'" (Acts 17:2–3, AT);
- "Paul was occupied by preaching, testifying to the Jews that *Jesus is the Messiah*" (Acts 18:5, AT);
- "By the Scriptures Apollos showed *the Christ to be Jesus*" (Acts 18:28, AT).

According to Scripture's own testimony, "Jesus died for my sins" is *not* the basic gospel message. As we'll see, the full gospel involves forgiveness. But if we build on an incorrect foundation, we skew the whole building. "Jesus is the Christ" is the basic gospel message in the Bible.

WHAT "CHRIST" MEANS

First things first. What does it mean to say, "Jesus is the Christ"? The words "Messiah" (from Hebrew) and "Christ" (from Greek) pertain to oil. Prophets, priests, and kings were anointed with holy fluid—oil—in order to be devoted for special purposes in the Old Testament (Exodus 40:15; 1 Kings 19:16; Psalm 89:20). God sent prophets to declare that a king would come in the future to restore his people (Isaiah 9:1–7; 16:5; Jeremiah 33:14–16; Ezekiel 37; Hosea 3:5). The hope for this Messiah-king crystallized around God's promises to David regarding an eternal throne for one of his offspring (2 Samuel 7:12–16; Psalm 89:3–4, 20–49; 132:10, 17). "Christ" is the New Testament word for this long-awaited anointed king.

Surprise! The gospel is political. This future Christ-king would not only lead over spiritual affairs but also exercise real-world *political* power to restore the fortunes of his downtrodden people. And not only his own people, the Jews, but also the non-Jewish nations, the Gentiles, would experience the effects of the Messiah's sovereignty. In this way, the Christ would be a universal king.

THE KING PROCLAIMS HIS KINGDOM

THE FIRST VERSE OF the earliest Gospel, Mark, links the gospel to messianic kingship: "The beginning of the gospel of Jesus the Christ, the Son of God." The gospel is about Jesus, the universal king. Shockingly this king also turns out to be God's own Son (see Chapter 4).

Since the gospel is about a king, it relates intimately to *the kingdom of God*. When Jesus first heralds the gospel, he speaks of the nearness of the kingdom of God: "Jesus came into Galilee proclaiming *the gospel* of God and saying, 'The time has been fulfilled, and *the kingdom of God* has drawn near; repent and believe in *the gospel*'" (Mark 1:14–15, AT). We'll discuss repentance and belief later (see Chapter 5). For now, notice that these responses to the gospel of the kingdom's nearness are not merely private religious decisions. They are political responses—with social implications—to the public announcement of a new king.

"The kingdom of God" was the time when God would rule overtly through agents that he would appoint—above all, through his Messiah. Although God always reigns, sometimes his rule is subtle, at other times obvious. Jesus proclaimed that an era dominated by God's explicit reign was emerging. Jesus could herald the nearness of the kingdom with integrity because he knew that the Messiah-king had just been anointed—himself!—at his baptism.

Although the Son was already chosen as Messiah by God, at his baptism Jesus became Messiah *within history*. Jesus received a holy anointing from heaven, making him "Christ." He was christened by the Holy Spirit rather than with oil. The Father confirmed Jesus' identity: "You are my beloved Son; with you I am well pleased" (Mark 1:11, AT).

Once Jesus became the Christ within history at his baptism, he could publicly announce the gospel of his emerging kingship, drawing from Isaiah:

> The Spirit of the Lord is upon me, because he has christened me *to gospel* to the poor. He has sent me to proclaim liberty to the captives and recovery of sight to the blind, to set at liberty those who are oppressed, to proclaim the year of the Lord's favor. (Luke 4:18–19, AT, citing Isaiah 61:1–2 and 58:6)

Jesus' Spirit-anointing as king was gospel for the people—especially for the poor, the blind, the oppressed, and the captives. This new king would be radically for the down and out.

Jesus anticipated an earthly political rule during a future era of renewal. When Jesus said his kingdom was not "from [*ek*] this world" (John 18:36, AT), he was speaking of its divine source or origin, not the kingdom's final outworking. (This is indicated by *ek* in the original Greek.) Jesus announced that in the age of restoration, he will judge and rule over earthly leaders (Matthew 19:28; compare Matthew 16:27; 25:31–46; 26:64).

The gospel was proclaimed by Jesus *before* his death. This hints that the gospel is about more than responding to what happened at the cross. Jesus summarizes his life purpose as gospel proclamation: "I must preach the gospel of the kingdom of God to the other towns as well; for I was sent for this purpose" (Luke 4:43, AT). Jesus proclaimed the good news that he was becoming the king. His anointing as king had set in motion a cross-and-resurrection-shaped process that would culminate in his complete, liberating, and cross-and-resurrection-shaped reign.

The church's main purpose today is to further this gospel announcement by declaring its fulfillment: *Jesus is the Christ*. Jesus has now been installed at God's right hand where he rules as the eternal king.

THE MISSING KING

BUT WE'VE MISSED IT. Although "Jesus is the Christ" repeatedly summarizes the gospel in Scripture, it is often absent from gospel presentations today. For to say that "Jesus is the Christ" or "Jesus is the Messiah" is to claim he is a royal *political* figure, *a human king*. (Albeit a divine king too.) We struggle to make kingship the most basic gospel category. It is not immediately obvious how a bare affirmation—Jesus is king—could be the essence of the good news. What about salvation? The cross? Forgiveness? The resurrection? We'll get to those in due course.

But first, we need to take the missing king seriously as a gospel problem. "Christ" has been reduced to a mere name, personal identifier, or alternative way of referring to Jesus. "In Christ alone," and the like, is the language we find in our songs and theology textbooks. To most Christians, "Christ" is equivalent to "Jesus."

Christ is a title. But to treat "Jesus" and "Christ" as equivalent terms is a huge mistake. On the one hand, it is true to say "Jesus saves" and "Christ saves." Likewise, one could truly say "Matt teaches" and "the professor teaches" because that accurately reflects my job title. But "Matt" does not mean the same thing as "professor." "Christ" is comparable to "His Majesty" if we're describing an English king. It is a special title designed to bring renown. "Christ" is the title for the universally significant Davidic king. Failure to treat "the Christ" as a title has contributed to a second reason why kingship has been missing from the gospel.

Forgiveness without kingship? Our haste to get what we so badly need causes us to misunderstand *how* forgiveness is available. What is foremost in our minds when we consider the gospel is a transaction at the cross: Jesus is savior, redeemer, atoning sacrifice, and lamb of God. Perhaps he has some vague authority too as Lord. We fail to see that forgiveness flows not just through a person, but through *a person in his official capacity as king*—crucified, raised,

FORGIVENESS FLOWS THROUGH A KING—CRUCIFIED, RAISED, AND REIGNING.

and reigning. While serving as king at God's right hand, he is also the high priest and the sacrificial offering that covers our sins. As will become clear, *Jesus' forgiving power cannot be separated from his royal authority as head of a new creation.*

THE KING DEAD AND RAISED

Although the foundational summary of the gospel in Scripture is "Jesus is the Christ," the most famous is 1 Corinthians 15:3–5. "The gospel" (1 Corinthians 15:1–2) Paul received and passed along faithfully to the Corinthians is:

> That the Christ died for our sins in accordance with the Scriptures, and that he was buried, and that he has been raised on the third day in accordance with the Scriptures, and that he appeared to Cephas [Peter], then to the Twelve. (1 Corinthians 15:3–5, AT)

Notice that forgiveness flows through kingship. Paul says nothing here about "Jesus." Instead, he speaks about *the Christ's* death for our sins. By mentioning the Christ rather than Jesus, Paul stresses that kingship is the vessel through which forgiveness flows.

Second, the king helps a whole bunch of people. Just as we short-circuit kingship in our haste to find *personal* forgiveness, we can easily miss how *the king's actions are group-oriented*. Paul says nothing about how you, I, or any other individual becomes right with God in this gospel summary. Rather, the king died for "our" sins. It's about what the Messiah has done for his *entire people*. Don't misunderstand. Benefits, like forgiveness of sins, that attend Jesus' kingship can be yours personally. But they are group-first benefits. Forgiveness belongs to individuals—you and me—only when we become part of the king's people.

Third, resurrection is gospel too. The Christ was raised on the third day. The validity of the king's death and resurrection was made doubly certain by God. For his death and resurrection were attested not only by Scripture (anticipated in the Old Testament) but also by historical occurrences. As part of the gospel, the Christ's death was confirmed by his *burial* and his resurrection by post-resurrection *appearances* to witnesses. The gospel includes the king's death for our sins, burial, resurrection on the third day, and appearances as historical events.

THE DIVINE AND HUMAN KING

IN THE TWO FOLLOWING passages, Paul offers gospel summaries. What are some emphases?

> The gospel of God, which he promised beforehand through his prophets in the holy Scriptures. This

gospel concerns his Son, who came into being by means of the seed of David as it pertains to the flesh, who was appointed Son-of-God-in-Power as it pertains to the Spirit of Holiness by means of the resurrection from among the dead ones, Jesus the Christ our Lord. (Romans 1:2–4, AT)

Remember Jesus the Christ, raised from among the dead ones, of the seed of David, according to my gospel. (2 Timothy 2:8, AT)

Both gospel summaries focus on Jesus as the royal Christ (or Messiah), his Davidic lineage, and his resurrection.

Concerning resurrection, there is something curious in both passages. They emphasize the king's resurrection not from his personal state of death (although he was personally dead), but *from among those who were also dead*. In the original Greek, the phrase *ek nekrōn* ("from among the dead ones") indicates that the dead king was with other dead people. Here's the point: if God raised him, he will raise others who are like him too. The king's resurrection from the dead is the first fruit, but a full harvest of additional resurrections will happen for all the king's people (1 Corinthians 15:20–22). King Jesus' resurrection is good news because it anticipates the resurrection of all those united to him through his death.

Let me offer a few more words about Romans 1:2–4 as a gospel summary. Paul takes a cosmic perspective. The Son took on human flesh, fulfilling God's promises to David. But God had a grander scheme. After the Son's death, his resurrection triggered his elevation to a new ruling office. The Son became *the Son-of-God-in-Power*. He has always been the divine king. But the Son has not always been a human king. Now he is the divine *and human* king, ruling creation powerfully. Since Jesus' reign in power pertains to the Spirit of holiness, his kingship is especially operative wherever the Holy Spirit is present. The Son's incarnation and enthronement are gospel.

THE GOSPEL PRECISELY

WE HAVE NOW EXPLORED the main summaries of the gospel in Scripture. If we were to add more, the most important are Peter's and Paul's speeches in Acts. Notice how Peter's gospel proclamation at Pentecost doubles down on Jesus' attainment of sovereignty: "Therefore let all Israel be assured of this: God has made this Jesus, whom you crucified, both Lord and Messiah" (Acts 2:36). Just as elsewhere in the New Testament, the cross is essential, but the gospel reaches its climactic energy with Jesus' rule as the Christ.

> THE GOSPEL REACHES ITS CLIMACTIC ENERGY WITH JESUS' RULE AS THE CHRIST.

When we bring together what the New Testament teaches, the gospel is about the process by which Jesus came to rule on God's behalf, restoring his glory.

The gospel is that Jesus the king:

1. preexisted as God the Son,
2. was sent by the Father,
3. took on human flesh in fulfillment of God's promises to David,
4. died for our sins in accordance with the Scriptures,
5. was buried,
6. was raised on the third day in accordance with the Scriptures,
7. appeared to many witnesses,
8. *is enthroned at the right hand of God as the ruling Christ,*
9. has sent the Holy Spirit to his people to effect his rule, and
10. will come again as final judge to rule.

Each event is repeatedly identified as part of the gospel in the New Testament. Elsewhere I've called this "the gospel-allegiance model."[2] But it's simpler to say these ten events are *the gospel precisely.* Above all, the gospel is the true story about how Jesus became the victorious, saving king.

REFLECTION & DISCUSSION QUESTIONS

1. If someone asked you what the gospel is, how would you define it?

_____

_____

_____

_____

_____

_____

2. What false gospel have you heard recently, either culturally or in the church?

_____

_____

_____

_____

_____

_____

3. Why is the simplicity of knowing the gospel and sharing it ("gospeling") so important in the Bible and now?

_____

_____

_____

_____

_____

4. When you discover that the gospel also proclaims the implications of the kingdom now, how does that apply today in political and social contexts?

_____

_____

_____

_____

_____

_____

5. As we've seen in this chapter, the gospel is more than just Jesus' work on the cross. How does that change your prior view of the gospel?

_____

_____

_____

_____

_____

6. What does it mean to you to accept as gospel that Jesus is king? How does that (or can that) change your life?

_____

_____

_____

_____

_____

_____

2

WHY DO WE NEED ROYAL GOOD NEWS?

Answer: God created humans in his image to rule. Sin distorts God's glory in our image-bearing. Only a king who flawlessly bears God's image can carry God's full glory to creation, vanquishing the personal, social, and cosmic effects of sin.

For all have sinned and fall short of the glory of God.
— Romans 3:23

Contemporary Christian culture encourages us to see the gospel as salvation instructions, but this is not an accurate view of the gospel. The instructions run like this: We need to acknowledge that because of Adam and Eve's sin, we all have a sin problem. As a result, you and I deserve death and punishment. God is by nature an impartial judge, so he is required to give us what we deserve. So death and punishment will be our fate sooner or later. But good news! God's fairness allows for substitution. Jesus was sinless yet carried your sins. Simply trust that Jesus died for your sins, paying the price for you. Then you can go to heaven.

These salvation instructions are not the gospel. We do have a sin problem. We are in a state of death. We do need to trust in Jesus as the sinless perfect substitute that provides atonement for our sins. And we can be united to his eternal life. As accurate as all of this is, in the Bible the gospel is about Jesus as the Christ. These salvation instructions only partially correspond to the gospel in Scripture because they do not feature Jesus' kingship. There is a disconnect.

The disconnect stems from an incomplete picture of God's purposes for humanity. The topic of sin helps us see why. What is so bad about sin?—after all, we are all sinners. Much is bad about it, in every way (Romans 6:1–2)! Yet when the gospel is incorrectly treated as personal salvation instructions, sin is one-dimensional. From this flat viewpoint, sin is only a problem because it *personally separates* you and me from God. This ignores the *social* and *cosmic* aspects of sin. To grasp why the gospel had—and must continue—to feature an actual *human* king, we need a bigger view of Scripture's story.

CREATED TO RULE

SIN DOES PERSONALLY SEPARATE us from God. Adam and Eve, after transgressing, are removed from direct fellowship with God.

But how does sin affect God's goals? What if God created humans for a purpose within his wider creation project—a purpose that is no longer achievable because of sin? What if God's aim in seeking to save sinners is to rescue them *for* as much as to rescue *from*?

> WHAT IF GOD'S AIM IN SEEKING TO SAVE SINNERS IS TO RESCUE THEM *FOR* AS MUCH AS TO RESCUE *FROM*?

Sin is not merely a guilt or debt problem that needs to be overcome to rescue us from separation from God or from death. Sin also prevents humans from fulfilling God's aims.

God's basic purpose for humans is announced in the first chapter of Genesis. God created the earth and universe as good. He created humans—male and female—and said they were very good (1:31). God made humans in his image, so that when humans rule over creation on God's behalf, God's own rule is made tangible and present to creation.

> Then God said, "Let us make mankind in our *image*, in our likeness, *so that they may rule* over the fish in the sea and the birds in the sky, over the livestock and all the wild animals, and over all the creatures that move along the ground." So God created mankind in his own *image*, in *the image of God* he created them; male and female he created them. God blessed them and said to them, "Be fruitful and increase in number; fill the earth and subdue it. *Rule* over the fish in the sea and the birds in the sky and over every living creature that moves on the ground." (Genesis 1:26–28)

Repetition makes it emphatic: three times in this short passage, humans are said to be made in the image—with it clear the *image of God* is intended. The purpose of carrying the image of God is *to rule* the various creatures, as well as the earth. We know ruling is the main human aim because God says it twice—first and last in this passage.

Scripture subsequently describes what this rule looks like. It is not coercive or enslaving. Adam is placed in order *to serve* (*'abad*) and *to safeguard* (*shamar*) the garden (2:15). After Adam's placement, Eve is given to Adam to be his helper (*'ezer*) in these tasks (2:18–22). If we miss that ruling in the Bible is about *serving* and *safeguarding*, we'll be endlessly confused about the royal gospel.

God's style of rule operates contrary to typical human expectations. We think a king should *be served* by his fellow creatures, that the ultimate king would place everyone and everything at his own disposal, his beck and call. If, on the other hand, God thinks kings should *serve* and *safeguard* creation, then the best king would . . . ?

Would what? If we are talking about the ultimate God-style king, *how far* would this king go to serve and safeguard? "For even the Son of Man did not come *to be served*, but *to serve*, and to give his life as a ransom for many" (Mark 10:45). Suddenly, the cross begins to make sense not just as a solution to the human sin problem. It is that!—but also more. The cross reveals who God is, and who we need to become.

BEARING GOD'S IMAGE

HUMANS ARE CREATED IN God's image to rule creation by making his glory present. In the ancient world of the

Bible, an "image" (*tselem* in Hebrew) was primarily a statue. Images were believed to make a god present.

Within Israel and surrounding nations, for worshipers of idols, the image did not just represent but was also a real manifestation of the divinity. That is, worshipers believed each "image" or "idol" of a god to be permeated with that god's presence, so that the god could appear to his worshipers at many locations at once. This is why different images of one and the same god could be placed in various temples but the worshipers could still feel that they were in the presence of that god.

For the convinced worshiper, the image made it possible to experience the god directly. More specifically, they could genuinely encounter *the glory* (weightiness, splendor, reputation, honor) of the god via the image. The image is what made the god locally present, so that anyone or anything in the presence of the image would necessarily experience *the glory* of that god.

From a biblical standpoint, images also make the one true God present. The Old Testament unilaterally rejects non-human *physical* images and idols of God. It is dangerous and wrong to represent God that way. At the same time, it endorses the image of God as an accurate and unique way to describe humans. Why?

Idols cannot carry God's image. Humans are forbidden to craft images of God out of wood, clay, and stone because they cannot make God present. As Scripture attests, the problem with idols is that people can't experience the glory of the living God through a mute, deaf, dumb, dead image (Isaiah 42:8; 45:20–25). That is, things crafted by human hands can't serve as an authentic place of encounter with God (Zechariah 10:2). At least, they cannot apart from being dignified first by Jesus' incarnation.[3]

Yet humans do bear God's image. Unlike dead idols that have no spirit (Jeremiah 10:14), humans make present the glory of the living God. Each human is permeated with the spirit/breath that God gives (Genesis 2:7), so they can make the living God's *glory* present in a local place. This is why in the midst of his words about image and ruling, God also commanded humans to be fruitful and multiply. Reproduction of humans bearing the image spreads God's glory to more locations (Genesis 5:3).

God designed us so that when other creatures, animals, or things encounter a human, God's glory is available at that place and moment. Psalm 8 explains: Humans are "made a little lower than *God* [*Elohim*]" (8:5, AT). (The Hebrew text says "God," but this may also include heavenly beings such as angels—see Hebrews 2:7–9.) As those made a little lower than God, humans have a glory that derives from God's own glory. They are crowned with "*glory* and *honor*" and given dominion over creation, so they can make God's glory available by their rule over it (Psalm 8:5, AT). When anyone or anything is in the presence of a human, God's glory—his tangible weightiness and splendor—is radiating outward through that human. Or, at least, it should be.

Disciple making highlights this point. Its goal is to help everyone conform to Jesus' image, as we reflect God's glory through the Spirit. Paul describes the purpose of his disciple-making ministry in 2 Corinthians 3:2–3 as crafting "living letters" written by the Spirit. He then describes the end result for disciples: transformation "into his image with ever-increasing glory, which comes from the Lord, who is the Spirit" (2 Corinthians 3:18).

SIN DISTILLED

ONCE WE UNDERSTAND WHY humans were made in God's image, we can see why Adam and Eve's disobedience is about more than personal separation from God. Humans are commanded to make God's glory present. Sin leaves creation bereft, so that it isn't experiencing God's glory. Sin results in a *systemic failure for all creation*. But what is sin's root? What is its essence?

God grants Adam and Eve access to all the trees in the garden but forbids one (Genesis 2:17). It is not an apple tree—it is the tree of *the knowledge of good and evil*. That is an odd tree. The strange specificity of this tree's description is of utmost importance for understanding sin.

In God's goodness, he tells us what is right and wrong. God defines human *moral behavior*, because he knows what will result in the ultimate good. But the serpent tempts: "God knows that when you eat from it your eyes will be opened, and you will be like God, knowing good and evil" (Genesis 3:5).

The fundamental human sin is to make our own moral choices apart from God's directives. This is sin distilled: God tells us how we should behave, but we do not trust that he has our best interests in mind, so we decide what is right and wrong for ourselves. Then we act on it.

Practically, the outworking looks like this: God gives a command, "Do not commit adultery." I think, for example: *Well, that sounds arbitrary. You see, there's this girl, and she needs me. And I need her. Plus, I know, God, that you say this relationship wouldn't be best. But I want this, and she does too. It's a messy world, so this choice is good enough given the circumstances.* So, based on this thought pattern, I act on my desire. I've just eaten the forbidden knowledge-of-good-and-evil fruit.

Adam is a model human. Each of us is born into his image and pattern of life (1 Corinthians 15:47–49; Romans 5:12). We do not fully trust God's directives with regard to right and wrong. We eat the fruit by creating and implementing our own ungodly moral standards. We do not deserve death because of Adam and Eve's sin; we deserve it for our own sins, because we freely make the same choice to violate God's commands. Again and again, each of us reenacts their fundamental sin in our own life story. The result?

THE MANGLED IMAGE

Like Adam and Eve, we have become like God, knowing good and evil. It sounds positive. But we are deceived. When we violate God's standard, we discover that God remains good but that we have joined *team evil*. Like God we possess moral knowledge. But ironically, this neither makes us like God in his goodness nor does it enable us to restore our own goodness. Quite to the contrary. We are naked, ashamed, and helpless in our sins. Our knowledge of good and evil exposes our moral ineptitude and embarrassing ongoing wickedness.

Meanwhile, God seeks us out, offering a path toward healing. God can ultimately turn our wrong choices to good (Romans 8:28). But unless we accept God's assistance, we remain separated from him, trapped in a vicious cycle of deluded disobedience. As the apostle Paul puts it, prior to and apart from the gospel, humanity as a whole is "dead" in "transgressions and sins"

(Ephesians 2:1). The effects of sin are death-dealing, grievous, and far-reaching.

Sin is personal. Personal separation from God is one problem caused by sin. Salvation includes restoration of a personal relationship with a holy God through Jesus' sinless offering on the cross (1 Peter 2:22–24; 1 John 3:5). But much gospel confusion is caused by a failure to move beyond the personal.

Sin is social. My sin problem is not merely my separation from a holy God. My sin is *your* problem—*our problem.* With some sins, like murder and adultery, it is obvious that personal sin harms other people and society. But private sins like jealousy or pride hurt other people too. They limit our ability to serve God and others.

Sin is cosmic. In response to Adam's sin, God announces that *the very ground* has been impacted. The pleasures of the garden give way to thorns and thistles (Genesis 3:17–19). The apostle Paul explains that the whole "creation was subjected to frustration" (Romans 8:20). In fact, it's worse, because the fundamental cosmic elements can be controlled by sin (Galatians 4:3, 9; Colossians 2:8). Even God's good gifts, like the Law of Moses, are perverted by sin, leading not to rescue but to death when pursued apart from the Christ (Romans 7:7–13). Although God made the old creation good, due to sin, it remains in such severe disrepair that it can't sustain eternal life.

Since sin is personal, social, and cosmic, sin's effects are *systemic*. This means its consequences are *universal within every system*. Sin impacts beryllium, balloons, banks, bombs, businesses, banquets, boyfriends, and your Aunt Bonnie. Everything. We desperately need rescue.

SIN CAUSES LACK OF GLORY

DOES THE BIBLE EXPLAIN why the effects of sin are universal and devastating? Yes, consider Romans 1:18–32. The systemic effect is not arbitrary. *Sin disrupts image-bearing, so humans and all creation have a deficit of God's glory.* A *human* king is required to restore glory.

HOW GLORY IS LOST

ALTHOUGH WE KNOW TRUE things about God through creation, we suppress these truths, because we would rather worship idols of our own making. We may not craft physical statues, but our idols are as prevalent and real today as in antiquity. Our most popular idols are the big three: money, sex, and power. Humans continue to worship idols, because they allow us to pursue our selfish body-centered appetites (Romans 1:24–27).

Paul bluntly explains how idols harm us: humans have "exchanged *the glory* of the immortal God *for images* made to look like a mortal human being and birds and animals and reptiles" (Romans 1:23). This glory exchange refers to the loss of our image-bearing capacity, as we turn away from God toward false images.

When humans worship images (idols) rather than the living God, they are swapping an encounter with God's glory for a bankrupt experience. When we make this exchange—and we've all made it—humans no longer fully carry God's image to one another or to the rest of creation, but we become like the false idols we worship (Psalm 115:5–8). Idolatry leaves us empty (2 Kings 17:5; Jeremiah 2:5), bereft of the fullness of God's glory. When we worship idols, the result is decreased exposure to God's glory, so that our derivative glory is not mutually refreshed when we encounter one another. Instead, we experience the opposite: a downward spiral into gross moral depravity ensues (Romans 1:24–32). When we worship idols rather than God, other humans and the remainder of creation fail to receive God's glory *through* us. We dishonor God too.

Given this is a universal human problem (apart from our union with Jesus the king), the slide into moral bankruptcy is fast and steep. Paul concludes his remarks about the human problem in Romans 3:23 with his famous words: "All have sinned *and fall short of the glory of God*." Notice that even though it is true that we are unrighteous, he does not say, "All have sinned and fall short of God's perfect standard of righteousness." Rather, Paul speaks about the lack of God's *glory*.

Paul wants to remind us that salvation is about more than a personal falling short of God's holy standard. We need the restoration of human image-bearing, *so that everyone and everything in creation will no longer lack God's glory.* Then God will be glorified by his creatures. This focus helps us to remember that our goal in the local church is Spirit-empowered disciple making, which transforms everyone more and more into the image of King Jesus.

WE NEED THE RESTORATION OF HUMAN IMAGE-BEARING.

THE KING RESTORES IMAGE-BEARING

We all need good news about a king because creation needs the restoration of proper human rule. God intends humans to carry his image to creation, so it can experience his glory. But image-bearing has become distorted by sin. We need a flawless *human* king who can restore God's glory amid humanity's brokenness. Then creation can be ruled by humans properly again and God can receive the glory that is his due.

REFLECTION & DISCUSSION QUESTIONS

1. This chapter describes sin as acts that distort God's glory. Share your understanding of sin prior to reading this chapter.

_____

_____

_____

_____

_____

2. How do you now view Jesus' kingship with respect to your need for salvation and atonement for your sins?

_____

_____

_____

_____

_____

_____

3. What does it practically mean for us to rule as God intended—serving and safeguarding?

_____

_____

_____

_____

_____

_____

4. How have you experienced the glory of the living God through another disciple of Jesus?

_____

_____

_____

_____

_____

_____

5. Disciple making facilitates spiritual transformation. Have you been discipled? Share your experience being discipled thus far in life. Have you made yourself available to be discipled and then to disciple others?

_____

_____

_____

_____

_____

6. What idols have you worshiped and what have been the ramifications in your life (spiritually, emotionally, physically)? How has God restored you in these areas to become his image-bearer again? What remains to be restored?

_____

_____

_____

_____

_____

3

HOW IS JESUS' KINGSHIP BENEFICIAL?

Answer: King Jesus frees us from our misguided self-rule. Christians alone have the benefits of forgiveness of sins and everlasting life with God. But as the king's glory radiates outward, non-Christians and the rest of creation profit too.

Salvation is found in no one else, for there
is no other name under heaven given to
mankind by which we must be saved.
— Acts 4:12

The gospel is *Jesus is the Christ, the universal king*, because salvation was never about rescuing humans simply for their own sakes. Salvation is for humanity's sake, for creation's sake, and for God's own sake—that he might receive the honor that he deserves.

This chapter explores key benefits of the gospel. The most obvious benefit pertains to the failure of my self-rule. I am not a very good king of my own life. I need King Jesus to lead me. So do you—and so does our troubled world.

Under Jesus' kingship, we are finally free to cast off our misguided self-rule—our pathetic attempt at life apart from God. Jesus' servant kingship results in full human flourishing. From Jesus we learn to reject inappropriate desires, handle wealth and its trappings, forgive our enemies, pray for those who persecute us, turn the other cheek, practice open-handed generosity, care for the downcast, and more. Jesus' Sermon on the Mount (Matthew 5–7) is especially revealing. It shows us a picture of life under Jesus' kingship. The benefits are countless.

> **UNDER JESUS' KINGSHIP, WE ARE FINALLY FREE TO CAST OFF OUR MISGUIDED SELF-RULE.**

Yet there are different categories of benefit. That is, the gospel helps Christians, non-Christians, planets, penguins, plants, and pencils—but not all equally.

A simple yet accurate way is to work from the narrowest to the most general. This suggests three categories of gospel benefits: exclusively Christian, human in general, and cosmic.

EXCLUSIVELY CHRISTIAN BENEFITS OF THE GOSPEL

THE GOSPEL HAS BEEN badly misunderstood if we think it helps only those who become Christians. The gospel is bigger than that. But the most important benefits are *exclusively* for those who commit to King Jesus.

Ultimate salvation is exclusively Christian. Jesus alone. "Salvation is found in no one else, for there is no other name under heaven given to mankind by which we must be saved" (Acts 4:12). Regarding eternal salvation, Jesus is not one of many possible ways, one form of the truth among many, and one solid model for life amid other equal options. As Jesus himself put it, "I am *the* way and *the* truth and *the* life. *No one* comes to the Father except through me" (John 14:6). Apart from King Jesus, there is no path to the Father, no road to eternal life.

For final salvation, Jesus the Messiah is the only way. But Scripture provides numerous ways to picture the rewards of this singular salvation: reconciliation, peace, union, atonement, redemption, becoming holy, enrichment, victory, triumph, exaltation, glory, rule, return from exile, rest, feasting, marriage, and life in the New Jerusalem. There are many more. But let's focus on four additional, distinctive Christian benefits of the gospel: adoption, right-standing with God, fruit of the Holy Spirit, and eternal life. These are vital to grasp for a full understanding of salvation, but are sometimes misunderstood.

Adoption. It's helpful to begin with adoption into God's family, because it is imperative to see the gospel's benefits are *for us* as a group—the church—before they are *for me* as an individual. God is creating a people, a special family, by the gospel's effects. That family existed before you and I were born. It will exist after we die. We get the opportunity to join it.

God's purpose to adopt a people is both timeless and timebound. In a timeless fashion, God chose the church as a group in the Son for adoption before creation (Ephesians 1:5). But that needed to be worked out in history. By the promises God made to the patriarchs, Israel—as a whole people—came to possess "sonship" (Exodus 4:22; Romans 9:4). Yet, since God's saving promises run through the king as a matter of history and fulfillment, these promises are ratified for Israel today only when Jesus is publicly acknowledged as Messiah and Lord (Romans 9:30–10:4; 10:9–10). In the wake of the gospel, Israel is saved only by faith in Jesus as the Christ. Non-Jews (Gentiles), although a

wild olive shoot, can be grafted into these family promises to Israel as these promises climax in Jesus the king
(Romans 11:17–27).

When this engrafting happens, non-Jews are adopt-
ed. The Father sent the Son for this express purpose,
"that we might receive adoption" (Galatians 4:5). The
result is that Jesus is not ashamed to call us brothers and
sisters (Hebrews 2:11). Through the Christ, everyone—
Jew and non-Jew—can join God's family.

Right-standing with God. A key benefit of the gospel is right-standing with God. This imagery refers to a
court of law. God is the judge. All humans stand guilty.
Yet through Jesus the king, this verdict can be reversed.
Sins can be atoned (that is, covered over) by Jesus' substi-
tutionary sacrifice. When an accused person is declared
"not guilty," they have joined the one and only family
that has right-standing with God, the true church.

The process of gaining right-standing before God is
called "being justified" in the Bible. The resulting sta-
tus is "justification" or "righteousness." Paul announces
righteousness as a core gospel benefit in Romans 1:16–17:
"For I am not ashamed of the gospel, for it is the power
of God for salvation. . . . For in the gospel the righteousness of God is revealed, righteousness that is by faith for
faith, as it is written: 'The righteous [one] by faith will
live'" (AT). The righteousness of God is a quality that
God's people can possess or enjoy (Romans 3:21–22;

Philippians 3:9). It is something God's people can become (2 Corinthians 5:21). The king makes "the righteousness of God" available "by faith." Here "faith" is best understood as going beyond *belief* or *trust* to include also *loyalty* or *allegiance*.[4] The king's people are forgiven and have right-standing with God.

Holy Spirit fruit. Not only do we gain right-standing with God, with the king's assistance, but we also make progress in becoming Christlike in our attitudes and activities. Part of the gospel is that the Father and Son have sent the Spirit to dwell within God's people permanently. The church is comparable to a temple of the Holy Spirit (1 Corinthians 3:16; Ephesians 2:22). Again, this gospel benefit is communal but personalized. At Pentecost when the Spirit was given to the community of disciples (Acts 2:1–4), it was experienced collectively (wind filled the whole house where they were sitting) and individually (separate tongues of fire came to rest on each). Likewise, the Spirit indwells God's people as a group (John 14:17; 2 Timothy 1:14), but each person who continues to confess, "Jesus is Lord," has a share in the Spirit (1 Corinthians 12:3).

The Holy Spirit guides the community into all truth, correcting, rebuking, and judging (John 16:8–11). The Spirit is the church's deposit, the down payment that guarantees its future salvation (2 Corinthians 1:22; 5:5; Ephesians 1:14). Those who remain attached to the vine—the king himself—produce fruit (John 15:1–5). Those detached from the king wither, die, and ultimately become fuel for the fire (John 15:6).

The fruit produced by the Spirit includes "love, joy, peace, forbearance, kindness, goodness, faithfulness, gentleness and self-control" (Galatians 5:22–23). In other words, the gospel benefits us because the Holy Spirit transforms us from fruitless to fruitful. The coming of the Holy Spirit is a foundational gospel benefit, since the Holy Spirit applies the communal benefits of the gospel to us personally. As disciples of Jesus, we are transformed so that we bear the image of Jesus in the fruit of the Holy Spirit.

Eternal life. This final gospel benefit is crucial but demands clarification. Scripture speaks frequently of "eternal life" (*zōē aiōnios*) as part of salvation (e.g., John 3:16; Acts 13:48; Romans 2:7). Yet this is not heaven. In fact, the Bible never explicitly says the gospel's purpose is to help a person get to heaven. On the contrary, as far as Scripture is concerned, the clearest statement of the gospel's purpose is found in Romans, stated the same way twice: "the obedience of faith" in all the nations (Romans 1:5; 16:26, AT). The gospel's final aim is not heaven but loyal obedience to Jesus the king in a new era—an era characterized by "everlasting life." Let me explain.

Heaven and eternal life are different. This phrase *zōē aiōnios* ("eternal life") is more precisely "era life" or "life characterized by the era." *Zōē aiōnios* intends life characterized by the kingdom-of-God era. This is the time period when Jesus reigns victoriously over sin, sickness, and death. It's an era humanity can enter right now (John 5:24–25)! Since in its fullness, this era includes the defeat of death and the presence of resurrection life, it is accurate to translate *zōē aiōnios* as "everlasting life." But unfortunately, this is easy to confuse with heaven. We are on steadier biblical ground if we say a key gospel aim is *everlasting resurrection-life* rather than heaven.

Scripture teaches about heaven and hell, but the topics are frequently misunderstood. They cannot be nuanced further here except to say heaven is best considered a holding stage in preparation for a renewal so dramatic that God says, "Behold, I am making all things new" (Revelation 21:5, AT). In the end, we won't go up to heaven; we are now waiting for the new heaven and new earth, which is when God's heaven comes down to us on earth. The heavenly city, the New Jerusalem, will descend like a bride prepared for her husband (21:2). It will be beautiful! The dwelling place of God will be with humans forever (21:3). Evildoers will be excluded. But all names written in the lamb's book of life will be included (21:8, 27). We will have everlasting resurrection-life as we reign over creation with the

King of kings (Revelation 22:5; see also Matthew 19:28; 2 Timothy 2:12).

GENERAL HUMAN BENEFITS OF THE GOSPEL

WHILE THE BEST BENEFITS of the gospel are reserved for Jesus' disciples, those who reject him are aided during their earthly life too—although in the end, they are excluded from final salvation. Jesus announces that his gospel brings relief for the poor, oppressed, blind, and captives (Luke 4:16–21). Non-Christians are better off due to Jesus' kingship because they experience social and political good when they encounter authentic disciples. The hungry get fed. The poor are aided. The cold receive a blanket. When the church acknowledges Jesus' kingship—and it always does when the real church gathers—they create an alternative social and political order that benefits the marginalized.

Delivery of these benefits to the marginalized can be hindered by wolves in sheep's clothing. These wolves claim Jesus as Lord, but their wicked deeds prove otherwise. In the end, Jesus will tell such people plainly, "I never knew you. Depart from me you evildoers" (Matthew 7:23, AT). The world is far better because of genuine disciples. But more often than we'd like to admit, the problem is not just the wolves. Followers of

Jesus, even the best, remain part of the problem. We do not merely stumble. We fall flat on our faces. At least, at times. How can the gospel benefit non-Christians, when even devoted Christians keep falling short?

COSMIC BENEFITS OF THE GOSPEL

INSTALLING JESUS AS KING, a human who perfectly images God, is key to God's rescue operation that benefits the whole universe. It jumpstarts a slow, lengthy salvation process for humanity and creation. *God's new-creation king initializes a restorative spiral upward of glory.* This is why Paul describes the good news as "the gospel of *the glory* of the Christ, who is the image of God" (2 Corinthians 4:4, AT).

The gospel's benefits are as wide as the universe because the problem is that wide too. We need deliverance not merely from the guilt that burdens us, but from the collapse of the old order. As Paul puts it, the Lord Jesus, the Christ, "gave himself for our sins *to rescue us from the present evil age*" (Galatians 1:4). We need to be brought into a new epoch.

In Scripture the old era ("this age") is under the sway of the evil one, "the god of this age" (2 Corinthians 4:4). God's first creation is reeling because the basic elements upon which it is founded have proven inadequate. *New creation* is the main cosmic benefit of the gospel.

Scripture's name for these old elements is the *stoi-cheia*. Paul speaks unfavorably of these elements, seeing them as enslaving: "When we were children, we were enslaved under the *elements of the world* [the *stoicheia*]" (Galatians 4:3, AT). Because the *stoicheia* can be controlled by sin to capture humanity, God had to do something dramatic: "But when the set time had fully come, God sent his Son, born of a woman, born under the law, to redeem those under the law, that we might receive adoption to sonship" (4:4–5). God had to free us from the old age by adopting us into his new-creation family.

Paul was distressed because some of the Galatians had turned back to childhood. They had re-enslaved themselves to the *stoicheia*, the foundational old elements, by performing the commands of Moses for right-standing with God. They falsely believed these works of the law showed that they were more right with God than others. But they'd compromised the gospel's result: one and only one justified family (Galatians 2:7–21). They were deeply misguided. As Paul states in the conclusion of his letter, God has established a "new creation," and this alone matters (6:15).

God's new creation ultimately can only be his work alone. But is this correct? On the one hand, it must be true. God alone is the creator of both old and new creation (Isaiah 45:18; 65:17–18; Revelation 21:1–5). Unlike God we cannot create from nothing. Humans can *rearrange* created matter and energy. But the matter and energy had to come from somewhere. So certain new-creation actions belong to God alone: God's establishment of fresh foundations for the universe, Jesus' resurrection from the dead, his enthronement at God's right hand, and the sending of the Holy Spirit to the church. These are all acts of new creation that God has already originated.

On the other hand, although God is the source, he uses humans to distribute his new-creation refreshment. God designed creation to be ruled by humans who bear his image locally within the world. Transformed disciples make God's new-creation glory present in the world.

The gospel provides benefits to Christians, non-Christians, and all creation. Through the process of Spirit-led image restoration, God transforms humans and then partners with them to bring his new-creation gospel benefits to all creation. What does this transformation look like?

IMAGE DEGRADATION AND RESTORATION

BROKEN MIRRORS—THAT'S THE result of image degradation. Shattered, fragmented, tarnished. If humans are no longer carrying God's image properly, then the whole created order lacks God's glory. You can't receive God's glory adequately through me, nor I through you, so it is never replenished. Failure in bearing God's glory is a vicious cycle, a spiral downward for humans and all creation.

"Image restoration" is the process by which the glory begins to spiral upward again. It starts with the incarnation. Jesus' incarnation is every bit as essential to the gospel as the cross. We cannot understand the gospel unless we see that the Son had to take on human flesh in order for God's glory to be restored. The restored glory of God in the lives of the people in the local church is the local church's goal in disciple making. Image restoration happens this way:

Step 1: Incarnate glory. God sends the prototype, his very Son, to become the human king. The Son is the pristine original image of God (Colossians 1:15; 2 Corinthians 4:4). When Jesus takes on human flesh, perfectly serving and safeguarding, humans are given the opportunity to gaze on the spotless image of God: "The Word became flesh and made his dwelling among us, and we have seen his *glory*" (John 1:14, AT).

Step 2: Transformed glory. As we willingly choose to gaze upon the Son as the perfect image of God, seeing his glory, we begin to be transformed. Again, Paul describes the process: "All of us who with unveiled faces are beholding as in a mirror *the glory* of the Lord are being *transformed* into *the same image* from *glory* into *glory*" (2 Corinthians 3:18, AT). As we turn away from the world and behold our king, we are being transformed by the Spirit into his image. Our minds are renewed (Romans 12:2). Our capacity to radiate God's glory is recharged.

Step 3: Conformed glory. We are increasingly *conformed* to the image of the royal Son (Romans 8:29; see also 1 Corinthians 15:49). The intensity of God's glory reflected through us to others increases. It's a group process. (This is one of many reasons why participating in church matters.) A cycle of recovery for humans and all creation ensues through mutual glory refreshment. As Paul says, in our present sufferings, we can scarcely begin to imagine "the glory that will be revealed in us"—a glory that renews creation in the midst of its present futile state (Romans 8:18)! Through renewed humanity, creation will finally be set free, "brought into the freedom of the *glory* of the children of God" (Romans 8:21, AT).

In sum, the degraded image of God within humanity had to be refreshed through an encounter with *the original image of God,* Jesus, in all his royal-servant splendor. It is our Christian destiny to be conformed to the image of the Son as part of our final salvation. This is the Spirit's new-creation work. As image restoration transpires,

THE DEGRADED IMAGE OF GOD WITHIN HUMANITY HAD TO BE REFRESHED.

God's new-creation glory is breaking into the midst of the old creation, reinvigorating it.

Yet the completion of our conformity to the Son's image awaits his climactic appearance, as does the full restoration of God's glory for creation. "We know that when he appears we will be like him, because we will see him just as he is" (1 John 3:2, AT). When we see the returned king in his full splendor, the church's image-bearing will finally be perfected.

All the benefits of the gospel ultimately flow through the new-creation power of Jesus as he rules at the Father's right hand. Jesus' incarnation, death for sins, resurrection, enthronement, Spirit-sending, and final rule are all gospel. The glorious king has broken sin's tyranny, allowing us to be true disciples who bear God's glory to one another and creation.

REFLECTION & DISCUSSION QUESTIONS

1. How would you describe the dangers of "misguided self-rule" to someone who thinks that being their own boss in life is the greatest thing ever?

_____

_____

_____

_____

_____

_____

2. Describe the uniquely Christian, general human, and cosmic benefits of Jesus' lordship.

_____

_____

_____

_____

_____

3. Of the four benefits of the gospel to Christians (adoption, right-standing with God, Holy Spirit fruit, and eternal life), which is the most difficult for you to accept and live out?

_____

_____

_____

_____

_____

4. As an authentic disciple of Jesus, how can you impact the general human population?

_____

_____

_____

_____

_____

_____

5. What does it look like to restore and refurbish God's creation? How can you participate in that?

_____

_____

_____

_____

_____

_____

6. How is "image restoration" a helpful description for God's plan for humans? What excites you about what image restoration could look like in your life?

_____

_____

_____

_____

_____

_____

4

WHO IS THE GOD OF THE GOSPEL?

Answer: God, who reveals himself through creation, showed himself specially to Abraham and his descendants. In the gospel, God revealed himself as three persons but one God: the Father sent his only Son, and they sent forth the Spirit.

> The Word became flesh and made his dwelling among us. We have seen his glory, the glory of the one and only Son, who came from the Father, full of grace and truth.
> — John 1:14

W e usually think about the gospel simply as what saves us. We do not ordinarily think of it as God's definitive way of revealing who he is. But the gospel unveils the Trinity. If we think that the doctrine of the Trinity is merely a tacked-on idea from subsequent church history, we've not yet understood the gospel. The Bible does not use the word "Trinity," but describes it in various ways.

THE TRINITY

TRINITY MEANS THERE ARE three persons—Father, Son, and Holy Spirit—but only one God. We see multiple divine persons but their deep oneness in Scripture. For example, Jesus stated, "I am in the Father and the Father is in me" (John 14:11), and "I and the Father are one" (John 10:30). How the three persons of the Trinity are one was clarified at the early Christian Councils of Nicaea and Constantinople in the 300s by using Scripture.[5] The three persons are one because they are the same substance or essence ("consubstantial" or *homoousios*).

The three persons are eternal. Each has always existed. But the persons eternally exist in different ways. Despite the various descriptions of the Father, Son, and Spirit in the Bible, in the final analysis, the eternal persons are only truly distinct in terms of 1) origin or cause and 2) the Son's incarnation (at least, that is all we can safely say).

How is each eternal person distinct with regard to their origin? The Father is uncaused (or unoriginated). Since the Christ (further described as the Son) ascribes the source of his begetting to God the Father long before Jesus was born in the flesh, we can conclude the Son is eternally begotten of the Father (Psalm 2:7; see also Psalm 110:4; Acts 13:33; Hebrews 1:5; 5:5; John 1:14). This means that the Father always has produced the Son in a fatherly fashion, and always will. Meanwhile the Father and the Son eternally send (John 15:26) or breathe forth the Holy Spirit (John 20:22). So in a timeless fashion, the Father is uncaused, the Father eternally generates the Son, and the Father and Son together breathe forth the Spirit.

The reason Christians by and large agree about the Trinity is that to deny it is tantamount to denying the gospel. The activities of these three persons are variously described in the Bible. But the gospel showed us clearly for the first time that God is triune. After the giving of the gospel, however, we can see hints in the Old Testament that God has always been more than one person. Yet the historical events that constitute the gospel are God's

THE GOSPEL SHOWED US CLEARLY FOR THE FIRST TIME THAT GOD IS TRIUNE.

definitive self-revelation in time: the Father sent the Son, and then they sent the Spirit.

WHO IS THE FATHER AS REVEALED IN THE GOSPEL?

IN TERMS OF THE gospel, who is God the Father? The one true God revealed himself to Abraham, David, and many others. God entered into *covenants* (legally binding agreements) with his chosen people. The oneness of God is announced clearly in Israel's covenant law: "Hear O Israel: the LORD our God, the LORD *is one*" (Deuteronomy 6:4). Then, when the time was ripe, God sent his Son, initializing the gospel.

Although Israel knew that there was only one God, the gospel revealed God to be the Father of a unique Son. And if we suggest that God wasn't the Father until the virgin Mary became pregnant with Jesus, we err. Scripture announces the Son preexisted with God and was part of God's redemptive plan *before* Jesus appeared as a man (e.g., Galatians 4:4–5; Romans 8:3; 2 Corinthians 8:9; Philippians 2:5–7). Moreover, if God only recently became a Father, then he fundamentally changed. But God does not change in such basic ways (e.g., Malachi 3:6; James 1:17).

Therefore, the events of the gospel showed that God must be at least two persons—eternal Father and eternal Son. We see evidence for this in the opening of John's Gospel: "In the beginning was the Word, and the Word was with God, and the Word was God. He was with God in the beginning" (1:1–2). This eternal Word (*Logos*) that preexisted with God the Father became flesh in the person of Jesus of Nazareth (John 1:14). The Father raised Jesus from the dead and enthroned him. At Pentecost, the Father collaborated with the Son in the sending of the third person, the Holy Spirit (Acts 2:1–4).

It would be misguided to detail the Father's unique saving role in comparison with the Son or with the Spirit. Except for special circumstances pertaining to Jesus' humanity (see below), when any one person of the Trinity is involved in rescuing, the others are also. In general, it is problematic to assign unique activities to the persons of the Trinity.

Consider the resurrection as a test case for mutual involvement. It is true that Scripture prefers to say God (the Father) raised the Son, since we find this affirmation dozens of times (e.g., Acts 2:24; Romans 10:9; 1 Corinthians 6:14). Yet Jesus also claims that he will raise himself: "Destroy this temple, and I will raise it again in three days" (John 2:19). Jesus was referring to the resurrection of his own body (John 2:19–22). The Father raised Jesus, but Jesus also raised himself.

The Son always participates in the Father's work. As Jesus puts it, "Whatever the Father does, the Son also does" (John 5:19). The Spirit was active in God's resurrection of Jesus and is active in ours too: "If the Spirit of him who raised Jesus from amid the dead dwells in you, he who raised Christ from amid the dead will also give life to your mortal bodies through his Spirit who dwells in you" (Romans 8:11, AT). The Father, Son, and Spirit are involved in one another's actions—at least, when those actions are directed toward creation.

So we must use caution when saying "the Father sent the Son," and the like, lest we give the impression this is the Father's work alone. The preexistent Son willed it too. The author of Hebrews reminds us, "When Christ came into the world, he said: 'Sacrifice and offering you did not desire, but a body you prepared for me . . . . Then I said, "Here I am—it is written about me in the scroll—I have come to do your will, my God"'" (Hebrews 10:5–7). The Christ as the eternal Son told the Father that he was voluntarily taking on a human body as a form of sacrifice, according to his Father's will.[6] In short, when one person of the Trinity acts to save, we cannot neglect the involvement of the others.

WHO IS THE SPIRIT AS REVEALED IN THE GOSPEL?

BECAUSE THE PERSONS OF the Trinity are involved in each other's actions, it would be wrongheaded to absolutize the unique function of the Spirit in our salvation. But broadly considered, Scripture describes the Spirit's saving activity in this way: the Father and the Son sent the Holy Spirit at Pentecost to the king's people as an end-of-the-age promise (Acts 2:17–21). *As God's new-creation power, the Holy Spirit makes Jesus' reign functionally present by indwelling the church in order to apply the benefits of the king's gospel* (see "Holy Spirit fruit" in the previous chapter). When an individual hears the good news about the king and responds, they join the ranks of God's people. This individual is immersed in the Holy Spirit, so that they have a personal share in the rewards that the king's people as a whole possess.

WHO IS JESUS AS REVEALED IN THE GOSPEL?

GENERALLY, WE MUST SAY that all the persons of the Trinity are involved in every saving action. Except! The Son's incarnation gives him a special role. The Son eternally preexisted as the second person of the Trinity, but became fully human in the first century as Jesus. But when the eternal Son united with Jesus' humanity, he did not cease being God. The gospel reveals Jesus to be both human and divine. Classically this is explained by saying Jesus is *only one person with two natures*—a fully human nature and fully divine (the Chalcedonian definition). Jesus is God and man—one hundred percent of each—all the time. Jesus, while remaining fully God, did not opt to use all his divine privileges, but emptied himself, for our sake—even to the point of death (Philippians 2:6–8).

In this way, Jesus on the cross is God and is God's ultimate self-revelation. The Son did not cease to be fully God when dying for our sins, so he showed us that to be God means to be selflessly for others. God humbled himself to such a degree that he died an agonizing death *for us*. God displayed an incredible depth of love for us—even while we were sinners (Romans 5:8; 1 John 4:10). For God to be God, and for us to be conformed to God's image, is to take up the cross willingly to serve and safeguard the well-being of others.

The Son's uniqueness as the only person of the Trinity to become human means that some of the saving actions announced in the gospel can be carried out *only by the Son*. Although all three persons of the Trinity were invested in the sending of the Son, Jesus alone took on human flesh. Jesus alone suffered for our sins by dying.[7] Moreover, although the Father, Son, and Spirit all hold the new-creation power of resurrection, Jesus alone was raised from death. Only he appeared to his disciples in his same real and tangible body—although it had been transformed as befits the power and splendor of the new creation that God is unveiling. Jesus was then taken up into heaven *bodily* while two men in white and his disciples gazed at him (Acts 1:9–11).

The bodily ascension of Jesus is vital for our salvation, for Jesus' *body* is part of the new creation. Mysteriously, Jesus is embodied still today as he reigns at God's right hand. Apparently resurrected bodies are suitably transformed so that they can exist in such a capacity. We know this because upon his ascension, Jesus was seated *bodily* at the very right hand of God, where he now serves as the King of kings (Ephesians 1:20–21) and our great high priest (Romans 8:34; Hebrews 8:1). Christians are *bodily* seated at God's right hand too, since we are hidden within our embodied king, who is resurrected and reigning from this position (Colossians 3:1–3).

Although the resurrected Christ, as divine *and human*, rules at the invitation of the Father, the Spirit is also involved. The Spirit makes King Jesus' rule functionally present (Romans 1:4; 8:1–17; 2 Corinthians 3:17). But the office of ruling as the divine-human King of kings belongs to Jesus alone. The *bodily* reign of Jesus at God's right hand is essential, for creation needs to be ruled not just by God but also by a perfect human who can restore humans. For ultimately creation must be ruled by humans who make God's glory present with their bodies. That is how God designed creation.

This is why among the persons of the Trinity, being "the Christ" is Jesus' office alone. It is essential that a flawless, embodied, human king rule creation, so that flawed humans can gaze on him in order to be restored in their image-bearing.[8] Then, they can make God's glory fully present to creation once more by ruling under and alongside the King of kings. This is why Paul, while speaking about the necessity of perseverance in the process of salvation, reminds us, "If we have *died* with him, we will also *live* with him; if we *endure*, we will also *reign* with him; if we disown him, he also will disown us" (2 Timothy 2:11–12, AT). Rather than disown our king, we must persist in confessing allegiance. Those who have *died* with the king will enjoy *resurrection-life*. Those who *endure* with the king will one day *reign* with him. Having been transformed into his glory-bearing image, Jesus' disciples will be fit to rule too.

For creation to reach the fullness of its glory, it must be ruled by humans: by King Jesus as he is assisted by his resurrected kings and queens. This is "the gospel of the glory of the Christ, who is the image of God" (2 Corinthians 4:4, AT).

> IT IS ESSENTIAL THAT A FLAWLESS, EMBODIED, HUMAN KING RULE CREATION.

REFLECTION & DISCUSSION QUESTIONS

1. How would you describe the Trinity to someone who hasn't heard the doctrine explained before?

   _____

   _____

   _____

   _____

   _____

2. Read Galatians 4:4–5. What does this imply about how long God has been the Father and how long Jesus has been part of the Trinity? For more clarification, see John 1:1–3.

   _____

   _____

   _____

   _____

   _____

3. How does the fact that the Son came to earth with two natures (God and human) impact your relationship with him?

_____

_____

_____

_____

_____

_____

_____

4. How do the two natures of Jesus work together to transform our lives?

_____

_____

_____

_____

_____

_____

5. We are image-bearers of God. The selflessness Jesus displayed in his dying on the cross is an example to us. How can you bear God's image as a disciple of Jesus in a more cross-shaped manner?

_____

_____

_____

_____

_____

_____

6. Read 2 Timothy 2:11–13. What does it mean to die with Christ? To endure with him? How have you personally seen others do these things?

_____

_____

_____

_____

_____

_____

5

HOW DO WE SHARE THE GOSPEL?

Answer: We share the gospel by testifying in word and deed that Jesus is the victorious, rescuing king. We encourage others to become loyal followers of the king through a faith response of trusting allegiance, repentance from sins, and baptism.

We are therefore Christ's ambassadors, as though God were making his appeal through us. We implore you on Christ's behalf: Be reconciled to God.
— 2 Corinthians 5:20

If only we could condense the shock, horror, beauty, and love of the gospel into an elixir. Then, we could bottle and pass it—astonishing!—to a neighbor, coworker, or friend. But God did not design creation's rescue, nor its rule, to work that way. For God's plan of salvation to reach non-Christians and the world, there is only one option: *disciples must function as image-bearers, testifying in word and deed that Jesus is the victorious king*. In response, hearers of the gospel are faced with a decision: Will they give allegiance?

HEARERS OF THE GOSPEL ARE FACED WITH A DECISION: WILL THEY GIVE ALLEGIANCE?

HUMAN TESTIMONY REQUIRED

FOR THE GOSPEL TO be effective, God needs not just Jesus but us also. Without humans opting to testify, Jesus' significance as the divine-human king would be lost in the mists of time. Fortunately, the apostles and others did bear witness—and in durable ways. The New Testament is largely the result of early testimony. Apart from the faithfulness of disciples of Jesus past and present, the gospel would never have reached us.

Bearing witness is key to the church's gospel mission. That is what Jesus told us just prior to his ascension. He described for his disciples *the way* the kingdom would be restored to Israel—and in so doing reach the world: "But you will receive power when the Holy Spirit comes on you; and *you will be my witnesses* in Jerusalem, and in all Judea and Samaria, and to the ends of the earth" (Acts 1:8). The kingdom will be restored through Spirit-empowered testimony that Jesus is the Christ. The early church grew by witnessing in this way. Likewise, testimony to King Jesus can fuel the church's mission today.

HOW DO WE WITNESS IN WORD?

To SHARE THE GOSPEL effectively, we must bear witness to Jesus as king in word, character, and deed. To many people, sharing *in word* can seem pushy or offensive today. Is it really wise? If so, how do we do it?

Words are necessary. We can't share through our actions alone. The beauty of Jesus' plan of restoration is that witnessing allows us to announce the objective truth clearly, but from a subjective vantage point that minimizes affront.

The objective side of proclamation. When I say that the gospel is objective truth, I mean its claims are not a matter of personal opinion—yours, mine, or anyone else's. Key gospel events are matters of history. As such they are part of the public record, open to scrutiny. We share the objective gospel with others when we tell them the ten events, what I've called *the gospel precisely.*

The gospel is that Jesus the king:

1. preexisted as God the Son,
2. was sent by the Father,
3. took on human flesh in fulfillment of God's promises to David,
4. died for our sins in accordance with the Scriptures,
5. was buried,
6. was raised on the third day in accordance with the Scriptures,
7. appeared to many witnesses,
8. *is enthroned at the right hand of God as the ruling Christ,*
9. has sent the Holy Spirit to his people to effect his rule, and
10. will come again as final judge to rule.

It is impossible to share the gospel without words because these ten events cannot be communicated by deeds or character alone.[9]

Since words are required, we should know these ten events intimately. So that you have a tool for sharing, I'd encourage you to memorize them. But then feel free to expand or contract, using your own words to share the gospel.

If you find memorization difficult, notice that the gospel has a story shape that makes it easy to remember:

It begins with the Son in glory with the Father. The Son became human, died on the cross for our sins, and rose. The gospel climaxes with Jesus' enthronement as king. (This is why it is italicized.) The Spirit has been sent. The Son will return to rule creation. In short, the gospel is the complete story of the Son, viewed from the lens of how God is using Jesus to bring about holistic restoration.

We must know the gospel well enough that we can tell it to others. Practice! But if you lack confidence or are afraid you'll forget something, don't worry. It is about sharing the good news, not following a script slavishly. Keep the *cross, resurrection, and especially Jesus' enthronement as king* in view. Then, trust, and share the gospel as the Spirit leads regardless of your fears.

The subjective side of proclamation. The genius of bearing witness to the gospel is that although the gospel refers to real events, it is always attested from a subjective (personal) vantage point. In announcing these ten events, I'm asserting that I'm *personally* committed to their truthfulness. In light of the testimony of others, I made a decision to acclaim Jesus as the king and by faith to give him my allegiance as his disciple. Now that I've done that, I've begun to enjoy the rewards. I can share how I've personally benefitted.

When sharing the gospel, we should be quick to add our own testimony to the validity of Jesus' kingship. This is especially helpful today because non-Christians are frequently sensitive to pushiness. I can say, "Let me tell you about my life." I can testify to how I made the mistake of thinking that I knew better than God in some area of life—money, relationships, sexuality, ladder-climbing, dealing with resentment. I can tell how I let someone or something else rule as king, at least in a season or a reckless moment. I can share about how I'm still struggling. Vulnerability opens hearts. Then, I can speak about how I came to discover (or rediscover) that Jesus is the only true King of kings—and how I'm still trying to learn it today.

I can then share the full gospel, the ten events, expanding on them or compressing as the Spirit guides. We can testify to the forgiveness he offers at the cross and his new-creation power, as evidenced by his resurrection and sending of the Spirit.

We add our own personal witness: I know that I am forgiven, created afresh, and imperfect but empowered, because of my life change. Above all, we need to testify to his present rule as king, and how allegiance to him

WE NEED TO TESTIFY TO HIS PRESENT RULE AS KING.

has led to partial but true victory for ourselves and others. We can share what it means to live day by day as his disciple. We can invite others to give allegiance too.

HOW DO WE WITNESS WITH DEEDS?

WORDS ARE REQUIRED FOR sharing the full gospel, but deeds and character reinforce its truthfulness. If I assert that Jesus is my liberating king and that I have become a new creature through the power of the Holy Spirit, but there is little or no evidence of this in my bodily activities, the claim rings empty. Hearers of the gospel's words will likely reject Jesus' kingship.

We all know hypocrisy undermines the gospel. But since we are all sinners and imperfect, isn't some hypocrisy inevitable? How do we tell people we've been genuinely changed yet remain honest about our ongoing sinfulness?

To answer, let's step back: Why would God use broken, sinful humans to share the good news? (Suddenly the elixir idea sounds more reasonable.) Unless God were to abandon his design for creation, it *must* be this way. Remember, the gospel is not a you-are-forgiven-so-you-can-go-to-heaven transaction. Creation requires human rule. Paul calls the good news "the gospel of the glory of the Christ, who is the image of God" (2 Corinthians 4:4, AT). The gospel is about a divine-human king who begins to restore God's glory by fully bearing his image. Since we all begin as mangled image-bearers and image recovery is a group process, it takes time. It will not result in perfection until we fully see the king. It is a spiral upward of glory restoration (see Chapter 3).

We can answer authentically by telling others that we are broken mirrors, trying to reflect glory, *while in the process of restoration*. Cracks and tarnish still exist. When saying this, however, deeds and character matter. If non-Christians cannot see a shimmer of glory in the midst of our brokenness—a glimmer that shows that the transformation underway is due to God and not us (2 Corinthians 4:7–12)—then they will likely reject the gospel. This is why our Christian deeds and character are integral to our gospel witness.

In sum, the primary way a non-Christian sees God and Jesus is to see God in you, me, or another disciple. If a non-Christian is to be saved, they must encounter a disciple (past or present) in the process of image restoration, who shares the gospel in words while giving a partial glimpse of God's glory in deeds and character.

HOW SHOULD WE RESPOND TO THE GOSPEL?

SHOUT, SING, PRAISE, DANCE. We should respond to the gospel with astonished gratitude and heartfelt joy! The gospel is God's grace (Acts 20:24). Sinful humanity as a whole did not deserve the grace of the gospel, but it is a gift that has proven effective for transforming sinners into the image of King Jesus. God acts first—and he has done this within history by the events that constitute the gospel—but human action is required in response.

We respond to God's grace by accepting the gospel of Jesus' kingship through faith, repentance, and baptism. Faith, repentance, and baptism are best regarded not as part of the gospel in Scripture. Rather, they are *how we respond to the gospel* in order to accept God's grace. Each connects to the gospel of Jesus' rescuing kingship.

Faith (*pistis*) involves *believing* certain things (the truthfulness of the ten events of the gospel) and *trusting* that the gospel is God's provision for salvation. But it goes further. Faith is not just mental; it is expressed with your body through relationships (Galatians 2:20; James 2:14–26). As a response to the gospel, above all faith is allegiance to your new king (e.g., Romans 1:2–5; 1:8; 1:16–17; 3:21–26; 2 Thessalonians 1:4–8).

Repentance (*metanoia*) is not just feeling remorse over your past sins. It is an active change of mind, heart, and behavior. Jesus calls those who want to follow him to repent (Matthew 3:2; Mark 1:15). Repentance is a *turning away* from wrong activities and sin-inspired loyalties (Acts 8:22). At the same time, it is a *turning toward* obedience to God and his rule over you (Acts 26:20). Repentance is a rejection of your old non-God loyalties as you instead submit to Jesus' kingship.

Baptism (*baptisma*) is a deliberate identification with the death, resurrection, and enthronement, not merely of Jesus but *of Jesus in his royal capacity as the Christ* (Romans 6:1–11). Baptism is said to be saving in the New Testament (e.g., Acts 2:38; 1 Peter 3:21), probably because baptism includes faith (Galatians 3:25–27) and is the definitive way to embody faith decisively. Some of our earliest descriptions of Christian baptism indicate that it included "calling upon the name" of the Lord Jesus (Acts 22:16, AT), which is best understood as undertaking an oath of loyalty to Jesus as sovereign.

After sharing the gospel, we need to summon hearers to choose. The center point of the decision is not whether to trust that Jesus died for your sins—for this distorts the *royal* gospel and misses the fullness of the required response. Rather, it is whether to give ultimate allegiance to the Christ-king. Once that decision is made, forgiveness of sins comes as a gospel benefit. The response is a call to salvation *and* discipleship into the ways of King Jesus.

Allegiance should be ratified through baptism. The best baptismal practices today will give ample space for the person being baptized to respond to the King Jesus gospel by repenting from past allegiances and declaring loyalty publicly. It should also be an opportunity for the gathered church as a whole to renew its allegiance.

TESTIFYING TO THE GOSPEL TODAY

A GLORY-BEARING DISCIPLE OF Jesus is shaped by the gospel pattern of life, especially the cross. A disciple should be prepared to testify about Jesus the king in word and deed. But doing this in our modern world is complex. Each age has opportunities and challenges. Four topics are especially pertinent to sharing the gospel today.

More than forgiveness. First, do not reduce the gospel to forgiveness at the cross. The cross is essential. But when we reduce the gospel only to what happened at the cross, we promote a self-serving parody of the gospel: personal rescue from a sin predicament so that the individual can enjoy the delights of heaven. The real gospel invites us to join the king's rescued people (the church), so that together, while being restored, we can serve others and creation in a cross-shaped fashion.

Responding to the king. Second, do not give kingship short shrift. If you haven't proclaimed to someone that Jesus is the Christ, the King of kings, then you haven't shared the full gospel yet. Moreover, if the king is missing, it is nearly impossible for the person hearing to respond accurately: Are you going to turn away from other loyalties and submit to his rule? The call to live as disciples of King Jesus rightfully realigns our entire lives. Disciples give allegiance to King Jesus and learn to align all we are and all we do under his authority and commands (Matthew 28:18–20).

Rewards and punishments. Third, do not be afraid to speak of judgment, rewards, and punishments. (On the benefits of the gospel, see Chapter 3.) Many are reluctant to bring up such things today—and let the Spirit lead—but generally reticence is unwise. Jesus and the apostles frequently taught about the punishments and rewards that surround this all-important decision (e.g., Matthew 13:41–43; 16:27; 22:11–13). Jesus is the pivot for individual and universal destiny. Everything is at stake. We should remind that the choice to follow or not follow King Jesus has tangible consequences—past, present, and future.

Yet I'd caution you when sharing the gospel against describing the punishment as hell and the reward as heaven, unless you can immediately explain further. Rather, speak of eternal separation versus resurrection-life with God. Heaven and hell are taught in Scripture, but these concepts have accrued cultural meanings that only partially align with Scripture's ultimate vision, so they need considerable unpacking. Talk about heaven and hell when appropriate. But even when opting for different language when sharing the gospel, it will usually be wise to emphasize the final judgment and the benefits/punishments—in this life and the next—that hang upon allegiance.

Incarnation matters. Fourth, make elements that have been neglected, such as the incarnation, a fresh opportunity. Consider how the incarnation is rarely featured when the gospel is shared but is integral to it. If you have a hurting friend, you can emphasize how God entered our hurt by becoming human through the incarnation. God knows and God himself has entered the full depths of our pain. Or share the gospel solution with a coworker who finds lack of respect for the environment detestable: God's placement of King Jesus as his fully divine *and human* image is the beginning of how God is restoring his *glory* over a renewed creation.

How can we share with a person who is convinced that they have already heard all this forgiveness gospel stuff before? When we explain why Jesus took on human flesh—not as a random fact but as an integral part of the saving gospel—perhaps we can get a fresh hearing.

Wanderers who find life purposeless may find their hearts stirred when they discover the gospel is not just rescue *from* sins but rescue *for* a fantastic purpose: they've been invited to join God's mission, to begin ruling under and with Jesus.

Good news! Let's tell others: Jesus is the rescuing king of glory, the King of kings.

REFLECTION & DISCUSSION QUESTIONS

1. What does it mean to "bear witness" to Jesus' kingship in word and deed?

_____

_____

_____

_____

_____

2. How comfortable are you in sharing the central historical truths in Scripture? Can you summarize or recite the ten gospel events from memory? Can you summarize them as a single story?

_____

_____

_____

_____

_____

_____

3. What is your three-minute personal faith story? You can start in the space here, if you wish, but I suggest writing this on a separate piece of paper or in a journal.

_____

_____

_____

_____

_____

_____

4. As a disciple of Jesus, what are some specific ways that your walk matches your talk? In what areas do you struggle with this?

_____

_____

_____

_____

_____

_____

5. What has been your experience in sharing your story of faith, repentance, and baptism with others?

_____

_____

_____

_____

_____

_____

6. How would you share the gospel's purpose, how it has touched your life, and the joy that it brings you?

_____

_____

_____

_____

_____

_____

_____

APPENDIX A

BOOK RECOMMENDATIONS FOR FURTHER STUDY

Matthew W. Bates, *Gospel Allegiance: What Faith in Jesus Misses for Salvation in Christ* (Grand Rapids: Brazos, 2019).

Michael J. Gorman, *Becoming the Gospel: Paul, Participation, and Mission* (Grand Rapids: Eerdmans, 2015).

Scot McKnight, *The King Jesus Gospel: The Original Good News Revisited* (Grand Rapids: Zondervan, 2011).

Paul A. Rainbow, *The Way of Salvation: The Role of Christian Obedience in Justification* (Milton Keynes: Paternoster, 2005).

N. T. Wright, *How God Became King: The Forgotten Story of the Gospels* (New York: HarperOne, 2011).

N. T. Wright, *Simply Good News: Why the Gospel Is News and What Makes It Good* (New York: HarperCollins, 2015).

APPENDIX B

RENEW.ORG NETWORK LEADERS' VALUES AND FAITH STATEMENTS

Mission: We Renew the Teachings of Jesus to Fuel Disciple Making

---

Vision: A collaborative network equipping millions of disciples, disciple makers, and church planters among all ethnicities.

SEVEN VALUES

RENEWAL IN THE BIBLE and in history follows a discernible outline that can be summarized by seven key elements. We champion these elements as our core values. They are listed in a sequential pattern that is typical of renewal, and it all starts with God.

1. *Renewing by God's Spirit.* We believe that God is the author of renewal and that he invites us to access and join him through prayer and fasting for the Holy Spirit's work of renewal.
2. *Following God's Word.* We learn the ways of God with lasting clarity and conviction by trusting God's Word and what it teaches as the objective foundation for renewal and life.
3. *Surrendering to Jesus' Lordship.* The gospel teaches us that Jesus is Messiah (King) and Lord. He calls everyone to salvation (in eternity) and discipleship (in this life) through a faith commitment that is expressed in repentance, confession, and baptism. Repentance and surrender to Jesus as Lord is the never-ending cycle for life in Jesus' kingdom, and it is empowered by the Spirit.
4. *Championing disciple making.* Jesus personally gave us his model of disciple making, which he demonstrated with his disciples. Those same principles from the life of Jesus should be utilized as we make disciples today and champion discipleship as the core mission of the local church.
5. *Loving like Jesus.* Jesus showed us the true meaning of love and taught us that sacrificial love is the

distinguishing character trait of true disciples (and true renewal). Sacrificial love is the foundation for our relationships both in the church and in the world.

6. *Living in holiness.* Just as Jesus lived differently from the world, the people in his church will learn to live differently than the world. Even when it is difficult, we show that God's kingdom is an alternative kingdom to the world.

7. *Leading courageously.* God always uses leaders in renewal who live by a prayerful, risk-taking faith. Renewal will be led by bold and courageous leaders—who make disciples, plant churches, and create disciple making movements.

TEN FAITH STATEMENTS

WE BELIEVE THAT JESUS Christ is Lord. We are a group of church leaders inviting others to join the theological and disciple making journey described below. We want to trust and follow Jesus Christ to the glory of God the Father in the power of the Holy Spirit. We are committed to *restoring* the kingdom vision of Jesus and the apostles, especially the *message* of Jesus' gospel, the *method* of disciple making he showed us, and the *model* of what a community of his disciples, at their best, can become.

We live in a time when cultural pressures are forcing us to face numerous difficulties and complexities in following God. Many are losing their resolve. We trust that God is gracious and forgives the errors of those with genuine faith in his Son, but our desire is to be faithful in all things.

Our focus is disciple making, which is both reaching lost people (evangelism) and bringing people to maturity (sanctification). We seek to be a movement of disciple making leaders who make disciples and other disciple makers. We want to renew existing churches and help plant multiplying churches.

1. *God's Word.* We believe God gave us the sixty-six books of the Bible to be received as the inspired, authoritative, and infallible Word of God for salvation and life. The documents of Scripture come to us as diverse literary and historical writings. Despite their complexities, they can be understood, trusted, and followed. We want to do the hard work of wrestling to understand Scripture in order to obey God. We want to avoid the errors of interpreting Scripture through the sentimental lens of our feelings and opinions or through a complex re-interpretation of plain meanings so that the Bible says what our culture says. Ours is a time for both clear thinking and courage. Because the Holy Spirit inspired all sixty-six books, we honor Jesus' Lordship by submitting our lives to all that God has for us in them.

Psalm 1; 119; Deuteronomy 4:1–6; 6:1–9;
2 Chronicles 34; Nehemiah 8; Matthew 5:1–7:28;
15:6–9; John 12:44–50; Matthew 28:19; Acts 2:42;
17:10–11; 2 Timothy 3:16–4:4; 1 Peter 1:20–21.

2. *Christian convictions*. We believe the Scriptures reveal three distinct elements of the faith: *essential* elements which are necessary for salvation; *important* elements which are to be pursued so that we faithfully follow Christ; and *personal* elements or opinion. The gospel is *essential*. Every person who is indwelt and sealed by God's Holy Spirit because of their faith in the gospel is a brother or a sister in Christ. *Important* but secondary elements of the faith are vital. Our faithfulness to God requires us to seek and pursue them, even as we acknowledge that our salvation may not be dependent on getting them right. And thirdly, there are personal matters of opinion, disputable areas where God gives us personal freedom. But we are never at liberty to express our freedom in a way that causes others to stumble in sin. In all things, we want to show understanding, kindness, and love.

1 Corinthians 15:1–8; Romans 1:15–17;
Galatians 1:6–9; 2 Timothy 2:8; Ephesians 1:13–14;
4:4–6; Romans 8:9; 1 Corinthians 12:13;
1 Timothy 4:16; 2 Timothy 3:16–4:4;

Matthew 15:6–9; Acts 20:32; 1 Corinthians 11:1–2; 1 John 2:3–4; 2 Peter 3:14–16; Romans 14:1–23.

3. *The gospel.* We believe God created all things and made human beings in his image, so that we could enjoy a relationship with him and each other. But we lost our way, through Satan's influence. We are now spiritually dead, separated from God. Without his help, we gravitate toward sin and self-rule. The gospel is God's good news of reconciliation. It was promised to Abraham and David and revealed in Jesus' life, ministry, teaching, and sacrificial death on the cross. The gospel is the saving action of the triune God. The Father sent the Son into the world to take on human flesh and redeem us. Jesus came as the promised Messiah of the Old Testament. He ushered in the kingdom of God, died for our sins according to Scripture, was buried, and was raised on the third day. He defeated sin and death and ascended to heaven. He is seated at the right hand of God as Lord and he is coming back for his disciples. Through the Spirit, we are transformed and sanctified. God will raise everyone for the final judgment. Those who trusted and followed Jesus by faith will not experience punishment for their sins and separation from God in hell. Instead, we will join together with God in the renewal of all things in the consummated kingdom. We will live

together in the new heaven and new earth where we will glorify God and enjoy him forever.

> *Genesis 1–3; Romans 3:10–12; 7:8–25;*
> *Genesis 12:1–3; Galatians 3:6–9; Isaiah 11:1–4;*
> *2 Samuel 7:1–16; Micah 5:2–4; Daniel 2:44–45;*
> *Luke 1:33; John 1:1–3; Matthew 4:17;*
> *1 Corinthians 15:1–8; Acts 1:11; 2:36; 3:19–21;*
> *Colossians 3:1; Matthew 25:31–32; Revelation 21:1ff;*
> *Romans 3:21–26.*

4. *Faithful faith.* We believe that people are saved by grace through faith. The gospel of Jesus' kingdom calls people to both salvation and discipleship—no exceptions, no excuses. Faith is more than mere intellectual agreement or emotional warmth toward God. It is living and active; faith is surrendering our self-rule to the rule of God through Jesus in the power of the Spirit. We surrender by trusting and following Jesus as both Savior and Lord in all things. Faith includes allegiance, loyalty, and faithfulness to him.

> *Ephesians 2:8–9; Mark 8:34–38; Luke 14:25–35;*
> *Romans 1:3, 5; 16:25–26; Galatians 2:20;*
> *James 2:14–26; Matthew 7:21–23; Galatians 4:19;*
> *Matthew 28:19–20; 2 Corinthians 3:3, 17–18;*
> *Colossians 1:28.*

5. *New birth.* God so loved the world that he gave his one and only Son, that whoever believes in him shall not perish but have eternal life. To believe in Jesus means we trust and follow him as both Savior and Lord. When we commit to trust and follow Jesus, we express this faith by repenting from sin, confessing his name, and receiving baptism by immersion in water. Baptism, as an expression of faith, is for the remission of sins. We uphold baptism as the normative means of entry into the life of discipleship. It marks our commitment to regularly die to ourselves and rise to live for Christ in the power of the Holy Spirit. We believe God sovereignly saves as he sees fit, but we are bound by Scripture to uphold this teaching about surrendering to Jesus in faith through repentance, confession, and baptism.

> *1 Corinthians 8:6; John 3:1–9; 3:16–18;*
> *3:19–21; Luke 13:3–5; 24:46–47; Acts 2:38;*
> *3:19; 8:36–38; 16:31–33; 17:30; 20:21; 22:16;*
> *26:20; Galatians 3:26–27; Romans 6:1–4;*
> *10:9–10; 1 Peter 3:21; Romans 2:25–29;*
> *2 Chronicles 30:17–19; Matthew 28:19–20;*
> *Galatians 2:20; Acts 18:24–26.*

6. *Holy Spirit.* We believe God's desire is for everyone to be saved and come to the knowledge of the truth. Many hear the gospel but do not believe it because they

are blinded by Satan and resist the pull of the Holy Spirit. We encourage everyone to listen to the Word and let the Holy Spirit convict them of their sin and draw them into a relationship with God through Jesus. We believe that when we are born again and indwelt by the Holy Spirit, we are to live as people who are filled, empowered, and led by the Holy Spirit. This is how we walk with God and discern his voice. A prayerful life, rich in the Holy Spirit, is fundamental to true discipleship and living in step with the kingdom reign of Jesus. We seek to be a prayerful, Spirit-led fellowship.

> *1 Timothy 2:4; John 16:7–11; Acts 7:51;*
> *1 John 2:20, 27; John 3:5; Ephesians 1:13–14;*
> *5:18; Galatians 5:16–25; Romans 8:5–11;*
> *Acts 1:14; 2:42; 6:6; 9:40; 12:5; 13:3; 14:23; 20:36;*
> *2 Corinthians 3:3.*

7. *Disciple making.* We believe the core mission of the local church is making disciples of Jesus Christ—it is God's plan "A" to redeem the world and manifest the reign of his kingdom. We want to be disciples who make disciples because of our love for God and others. We personally seek to become more and more like Jesus through his Spirit so that Jesus would live through us. To help us focus on Jesus, his sacrifice on the cross, our unity in him, and his coming return, we typically share

communion in our weekly gatherings. We desire the fruits of biblical disciple making which are disciples who live and love like Jesus and "go" into every corner of society and to the ends of the earth. Disciple making is the engine that drives our missional service to those outside the church. We seek to be known where we live for the good that we do in our communities. We love and serve all people, as Jesus did, no strings attached. At the same time, as we do good for others, we also seek to form relational bridges that we prayerfully hope will open doors for teaching people the gospel of the kingdom and the way of salvation.

> *Matthew 28:19–20; Galatians 4:19;*
> *Acts 2:41; Philippians 1:20–21; Colossians 1:27–29;*
> *2 Corinthians 3:3; 1 Thessalonians 2:19–20;*
> *John 13:34–35; 1 John 3:16; 1 Corinthians 13:1–13;*
> *Luke 22:14–23; 1 Corinthians 11:17–24; Acts 20:7.*

8. *Kingdom life.* We believe in the present kingdom reign of God, the power of the Holy Spirit to transform people, and the priority of the local church. God's holiness should lead our churches to reject lifestyles characterized by pride, sexual immorality, homosexuality, easy divorce, idolatry, greed, materialism, gossip, slander, racism, violence, and the like. God's love should lead our churches to emphasize love as the distinguishing sign of

a true disciple. Love for one another should make the church like an extended family—a fellowship of married people, singles, elderly, and children who are all brothers and sisters to one another. The love of the extended church family to one another is vitally important. Love should be expressed in both service to the church and to the surrounding community. It leads to the breaking down of walls (racial, social, political), evangelism, acts of mercy, compassion, forgiveness, and the like. By demonstrating the ways of Jesus, the church reveals God's kingdom reign to the watching world.

1 Corinthians 1:2; Galatians 5:19–21;
Ephesians 5:3–7; Colossians 3:5–9;
Matthew 19:3–12; Romans 1:26–32; 14:17–18;
1 Peter 1:15–16; Matthew 25:31–46;
John 13:34–35; Colossians 3:12–13; 1 John 3:16;
1 Corinthians 13:1–13; 2 Corinthians 5:16–21.

9. *Counter-cultural living*. We believe Jesus' Lordship through Scripture will lead us to be a distinct light in the world. We follow the first and second Great Commandments where love and loyalty to God come first and love for others comes second. So we prioritize the gospel and one's relationship with God, with a strong commitment to love people in their secondary points of need too. The gospel is God's light for us. It teaches us

grace, mercy, and love. It also teaches us God's holiness, justice, and the reality of hell which led to Jesus' sacrifice of atonement for us. God's light is grace and truth, mercy and righteousness, love and holiness. God's light among us should be reflected in distinctive ways like the following:

A. We believe that human life begins at conception and ends upon natural death, and that all human life is priceless in the eyes of God. All humans should be treated as image-bearers of God. For this reason, we stand for the sanctity of life both at its beginning and its end. We oppose elective abortions and euthanasia as immoral and sinful. We understand that there are very rare circumstances that may lead to difficult choices when a mother or child's life is at stake, and we prayerfully surrender and defer to God's wisdom, grace, and mercy in those circumstances.

B. We believe God created marriage as the context for the expression and enjoyment of sexual relations. Jesus defines marriage as a covenant between one man and one woman. We believe that all sexual activity outside the bounds of marriage, including same-sex unions and same-sex marriage, are immoral and must not be condoned by disciples of Jesus.

C. We believe that Jesus invites all races and ethnicities into the kingdom of God. Because humanity has exhibited grave racial injustices throughout history, we believe that everyone, especially disciples, must be proactive in securing justice for people of all races and that racial reconciliation must be a priority for the church.

D. We believe that both men and women were created by God to equally reflect, in gendered ways, the nature and character of God in the world. In marriage, husbands and wives are to submit to one another, yet there are gender specific expressions: husbands model themselves in relationship with their wives after Jesus' sacrificial love for the church, and wives model themselves in relationship with their husbands after the church's willingness to follow Jesus. In the church, men and women serve as partners in the use of their gifts in ministry, while seeking to uphold New Testament norms which teach that the lead teacher/preacher role in the gathered church and the elder/overseer role are for qualified men. The vision of the Bible is an equal partnership of men and women in creation, in marriage, in salvation, in the gifts of the Spirit, and in the ministries of the church but exercised in ways that honor gender as described in the Bible.

E. We believe that we must resist the forces of culture that focus on materialism and greed. The Bible teaches that the love of money is the root of all sorts of evil and that greed is idolatry. Disciples of Jesus should joyfully give liberally and work sacrificially for the poor, the marginalized, and the oppressed.

Romans 12:3–8; Matthew 22:36–40; 1 Corinthians 12:4–7; Ephesians 2:10; 4:11–13; 1 Peter 4:10–11; Matthew 20:24–27; Philippians 1:1; Acts 20:28; 1 Timothy 2:11–15; 3:1–7; Titus 1:5–9; 1 Corinthians 11:2–9; 14:33–36; Ephesians 5:21–33; Colossians 3:18–19; 1 Corinthians 7:32–35.

10. *The end.* We believe that Jesus is coming back to earth in order to bring this age to an end. Jesus will reward the saved and punish the wicked, and finally destroy God's last enemy, death. He will put all things under the Father, so that God may be all in all forever. That is why we have urgency for the Great Commission—to make disciples of all nations. We like to look at the Great Commission as an inherent part of God's original command to "be fruitful and multiply."

We want to be disciples of Jesus who love people and help them to be disciples of Jesus. We are a movement of disciples who make disciples who help renew existing churches and who start new churches that make more disciples. We want to reach as many as possible—until Jesus returns and God restores all creation to himself in the new heaven and new earth.

Matthew 25:31–32; Acts 17:31; Revelation 20:11–15; 2 Thessalonians 1:6–10; Mark 9:43–49; Luke 12:4–7; Acts 4:12; John 14:6; Luke 24:46–48; Matthew 28:19–20; Genesis 12:1–3; Galatians 2:20; 4:19; Luke 6:40; Luke 19:10; Revelation 21:1ff.

NOTES

1. For a fuller development of the central ideas in this chapter, see Matthew W. Bates, *Gospel Allegiance* (Grand Rapids: Brazos, 2019), 40–54, 86–104.

2. This ten-event consolidation of the gospel is drawn verbatim from Matthew W. Bates, *Gospel Allegiance* (Grand Rapids: Brazos, 2019), 86–87. Point 8 is italicized because it is the climax of the gospel in the New Testament. The events are given expanded treatment on pages 87–104.

3. Today most Christians agree that through Jesus' incarnation, God dignified the whole created order so that physical materials can now be used to make icons of Jesus and other holy people as an aid. These icons can be reverenced but not worshiped. The story of how most Christians came to this agreement relates to the resolution of an eighth and ninth-century dispute called the iconoclast controversy.

4. The Greek word *pistis* (traditionally translated "faith") is better translated "faithfulness," "fidelity,"

"loyalty," or "allegiance" in Romans 1:17 (and also in 1:5; 1:8; 1:12; 3:3; 3:22; and other passages). In Romans 1:17, "by *pistis*" refers to Jesus the king's faithful loyalty to God and "for *pistis*" refers to our faithful loyalty to Jesus as the king. For discussion, see Bates, *Gospel Allegiance*, 73–82.

5. See Matthew W. Bates, *The Birth of the Trinity: Jesus, God, and Spirit in New Testament and Early Christian Interpretations of the Old Testament* (Oxford: Oxford University Press, 2015).

6. Since Hebrews 10:5–7 quotes Psalm 40:7–9, this is one of those intriguing Old Testament passages that, in light of the gospel, hints that God is more than one person. For discussion, see Bates, *The Birth of the Trinity*, 85–87.

7. In fact, to say that the Father suffered on the cross is a heresy the early church rejected called "Patripassianism."

8. For a more in-depth discussion of the essentials of the Christian faith, as well as of its important elements and personal elements, see Chad Ragsdale, *Christian Convictions: Discerning the Essential, Important, and Personal Elements* (Renew.org, 2021).

9. This gospel definition is from Bates, *Gospel Allegiance*, 86–87. On sharing the gospel, see Bates, *Salvation by Allegiance Alone* (Grand Rapids: Baker Academic, 2017), 198–210.

Made in United States
North Haven, CT
08 November 2023

43791900R00076